Just Say Hello

© Copyright 2023 Jennifer Hartinger
All rights reserved
ISBN Paperback: 978-0-9964588-63
ISBN Hardcover: 978-0-9964588-70

For additional or signed copies,
please visit www.jenniferhartinger.com

Dedicated to all those kids
who are battling cancer and
everyone who supports them.

This book belongs to

LET ME TELL YOU A STORY
about
a girl named Nicole.
Her story needs to be told
if I can be so bold.

She may not look like you,
but she is you.
She gets happy and sad
and sometimes mad.

She was happy those days
when all she did was play
and sad the day the
doctor said, "Not today!"

He wasn't a mean doctor;
he was her friend.
But he was trying to heal her
and help her mend.

You see she was sick
and not even six.
She had cancer, he said,
and needed to be in bed.

Cancer

She was in the fight for her life
with family by her side.
They were ready to battle
and took it in stride.

Nicole didn't know
what was happening,
but her mom started to cry.
So, she did what they said
with a tear in her eye.

They told her about treatments,
and she needed to fight.
So that's what she did
with all her might.

Her hair fell out and
her body became weak.
Some strangers started
to stare in disbelief.

16

She tried to wear wigs
to look like the other kids.
But they all itched her head,
so she wore bandannas instead.

Soccer was her thing;
it made her heart sing.
When she took to the field,
she felt like a queen.

Her teammates, in support,
wore bandannas like Nicole's,
which definitely touched
everyone's soul.

How could she play soccer
with her body being weak?
But her coach put her
in positions where she
could play and compete.

Nicole slowly was learning
a new way of living
and decided to help
the animals by spending
some time giving.

She sold lemonade
at the end of her pier
to help the seals
who lived so near.

Nicole's mom went to her class
and spoke with her friends.
She gave them advice
on how to help her daughter mend.

Her mom said,
"This is something that you may not know,
but the best way to support Nicole
is just say "hello."

Just Say Hello

The next day at school
her friends said, "Hello."
Suddenly you could see
Nicole smile and glow.

Her mom said to her class,
"Please pass this along
because kids that are different
just want to belong."

Say ∞ Hello

It's really that simple
and easy to see
how just saying hello
can help you and me.

This story has ended,
but cancer has not.
Nicole was very fortunate
to have won her battle with
cancer and is now a healthy
thriving young adult.

Please, if you can support
hospitals and charities
that help families
fight cancer, that would
be great! Because every
little bit helps.

Just Say Hello

About the Author

Jennifer Hartinger is a writer from Long Beach, California. A graduate of the Walter Cronkite School of Broadcast Journalism, her earlier books include *A Girl Named Sam*, *A Boy Named Bill*, and *A Dog Named Lou*. She also enjoys writing comedy online with credits on several comedy websites as well as *The Tonight Show*.

About the Illustrator

Ann Hoekstra is an illustrator who specializes in creating engaging artwork and graphics. Her illustrations focus on a richness of texture and she strives to create engaging and lively characters in her work. *Just Say Hello* is Ann's first book.

About the Designer

Jennifer Adler is a freelance graphic designer living and working in Lynn, Massachusetts. A graduate of Rhode Island School of Design and Brandeis University, Jennifer enjoys reading special books like this one to her daughter. *Just Say Hello* is her second book with Jennifer Hartinger.